1985

The damage to the ozone layer over Antarctica is first reported by scientists.

2003

A heat wave and drought across much of Europe leaves as many as 70,000 dead.

1975

Typhoon Nina hits China, destroying a series of dams and causing more than 100,000 deaths.

2005

Hurricane Katrina batters Louisiana, flooding much of New Orleans. It kills more than 1,800 people and causes more than $80 billion worth of damage.

1989

A tornado destroys two towns in the Manikganj district of Bangladesh, killing an estimated 1,300 people in a few minutes.

Extreme Weather Around the World

Human beings have a remarkable knack for overcoming all sorts of difficult conditions. People all over the world have learned to cope with —and even make use of—extreme weather.

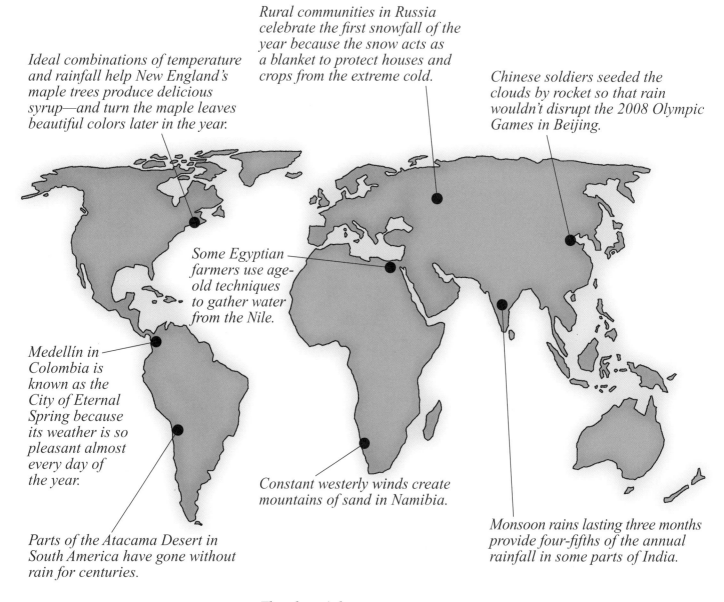

Rural communities in Russia celebrate the first snowfall of the year because the snow acts as a blanket to protect houses and crops from the extreme cold.

Ideal combinations of temperature and rainfall help New England's maple trees produce delicious syrup—and turn the maple leaves beautiful colors later in the year.

Chinese soldiers seeded the clouds by rocket so that rain wouldn't disrupt the 2008 Olympic Games in Beijing.

Some Egyptian farmers use age-old techniques to gather water from the Nile.

Medellín in Colombia is known as the City of Eternal Spring because its weather is so pleasant almost every day of the year.

Constant westerly winds create mountains of sand in Namibia.

Parts of the Atacama Desert in South America have gone without rain for centuries.

Monsoon rains lasting three months provide four-fifths of the annual rainfall in some parts of India.

The planet's lowest temperatures were recorded at the Vostok research station in Antarctica.

Author:

Roger Canavan is an accomplished author who has written, edited, and contributed to more than a dozen books about science and other educational subjects. His three children are his sternest critics—and his fellow explorers in the pursuit of knowledge.

Artist:

Mark Bergin was born in Hastings, England, in 1961. He studied at Eastbourne College of Art and specializes in historical reconstructions, aviation, and maritime subjects. He lives in Bexhill-on-Sea with his wife and children.

Series creator:

David Salariya was born in Dundee, Scotland. He has illustrated a wide range of books and has created and designed many new series for publishers in the UK and overseas. David established The Salariya Book Company in 1989. He lives in Brighton, England, with his wife, illustrator Shirley Willis, and their son, Jonathan.

Editor: **Stephen Haynes**

Editorial Assistant: **Rob Walker**

Published in Great Britain in 2015 by
The Salariya Book Company Ltd
25 Marlborough Place, Brighton BN1 1UB

ISBN-13: 978-0-531-21365-0 (lib. bdg.) 978-0-531-21408-4 (pbk.)

All rights reserved.
Published in 2015 in the United States
by Franklin Watts
An imprint of Scholastic Inc.
Published simultaneously in Canada.

A CIP catalog record for this book is available
from the Library of Congress.

Printed and bound in Shenzhen, China.
Printed on paper from sustainable sources.
Reprinted in MMXV.
2 3 4 5 6 7 8 9 10 R 24 23 22 21 20 19 18 17 16 15

PAPER FROM
SUSTAINABLE
FORESTS

You Wouldn't Want to Live Without™

Extreme Weather!

Written by
Roger Canavan

Illustrated by
Mark Bergin

Created and designed by
David Salariya

Franklin Watts®
An Imprint of Scholastic Inc.
NEW YORK • TORONTO • LONDON • AUCKLAND • SYDNEY
MEXICO CITY • NEW DELHI • HONG KONG
DANBURY, CONNECTICUT

Contents

Introduction

Everyone seems to be interested in the weather, and the kind of weather that makes people really want to talk is the extreme kind. Extreme weather can be unusually hot or extremely cold. It can be incredibly wet or as dry as dust.

Most of the time, people sigh with relief when a period of extreme weather is over. They hope that they can get on with "normal" life, and that normal weather will be part of it. Yet many people depend on extreme weather. They may hope for four straight months of rain for their rice crop, or for a cold winter so that next year's apples will be more plentiful. And extreme weather in one place may be useful somewhere else: If the North and South Poles were not extremely cold, the polar ice would melt and many island nations would be flooded.

Is Weather the Same as Climate?

The words *weather* and *climate* both describe the same kinds of things—blizzards, heat waves, or hurricanes—so you might think they have the same meaning. But they are different things, and the difference is really quite easy to understand. It's all about time.

Weather describes conditions around you over a relatively short time—an hour, a day, or a week. Weather can arrive or change unexpectedly. *Climate* describes what the weather is usually like over a period of many years. It's more predictable than weather. Or, as one weather scientist put it, "Climate is what you expect, but weather is what you get."

MONSOONS are intense periods of rain that last for months. The southwest monsoon in India provides 80 percent of the country's annual rainfall in just three months. It's an extreme, but predictable, part of the climate.

WE ALL KNOW what the climate is like where we live. That's why we're surprised when we see weather that's unexpected—like winter snow in a place with a warm climate.

Water makes its way around our planet in a pattern called the water cycle. Warm air causes ocean water to evaporate and form clouds. As clouds get higher, they cool and the water falls as rain. Much of it runs off as streams and rivers until it reaches the sea again.

Water vapor

Rain

Runoff

CHILDREN in many American cities may get a chance to have a refreshing shower from a fire hydrant during the hottest days of summer. The hot weather is not a big surprise, because it happens most years—it's part of the climate of those cities. The parents of these children probably used to cool down in the same way when they were young.

MUCH OF OUR WEATHER develops over the oceans, which cover more than two-thirds of the planet. Warm air can suck up water from the sea to become clouds—and then rain.

GOVERNMENTS AND OFFICIALS need to be aware of the climate so that they are prepared for weather emergencies. People in cold climates make sure that their snow-clearing equipment is ready all winter.

What If the Weather Never Changed?

It's tempting to look out at the rain and think that life would be so much better if it never rained. Or maybe you're making a snowman and think, "I wish this winter would go on forever."

In some parts of the world, though, the weather really does remain almost the same all year long, year after year.

When you've gotten used to that idea, you might wonder what life would be like if everywhere on Earth had the same weather and climate. Now that's a different matter altogether, and you'll see how much we all need that variation.

PARTS OF THE ATACAMA DESERT in Chile have had no recorded rain for 400 years. The air on the west coast is dry, and any rain coming in from the east falls on mountains before it reaches the desert.

RICE IS GROWN in flooded fields called paddies. But this important grain needs more than just lots of water. A special combination of heat, sunshine, and rainfall—in other words, the right weather—gets the best results.

You Can Do It!

For a month, record what the weather is each day when you wake up. See how often it changes—even if you think it's "normal." If you're really patient, you can record the same month next year. Can you see some patterns that give you clues about the climate?

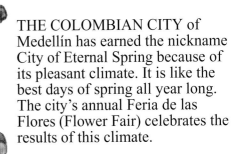

THE COLOMBIAN CITY of Medellín has earned the nickname City of Eternal Spring because of its pleasant climate. It is like the best days of spring all year long. The city's annual Feria de las Flores (Flower Fair) celebrates the results of this climate.

THE EARLY SPRING weather conditions have to be just right for the sap to run freely in the sugar maple trees of New England, in the United States, and Canada. But when it does flow, it can be boiled down to make maple syrup.

APPLES and many other plants need frosts and periods of cold during the winter so that their fruit can develop. If it were "eternal spring" around the world, you'd never see another apple.

Can Electrical Storms Help Us?

The rolling boom of thunder and the bright flash of lightning often occur during a powerful storm. A thunderstorm is sometimes called an electrical storm, because the lightning is an incredibly powerful electric charge. (American scientist and statesman Benjamin Franklin proved this in 1752, in a very dangerous experiment involving a key tied to a kite string.) A lightning bolt carves a tunnel through the air as it rushes down from a cloud. Hot air around the lightning expands quickly, producing vibrations that create the sound of thunder. Light travels much, much faster than sound. That's why we often see the lightning first, then a few seconds later we hear the thunder.

Cra-a-ack!

A THUNDERSTORM in a big city is a dramatic sight, with lightning striking the tops of skyscrapers. All tall buildings are fitted with a lightning rod, a metal strip that leads the electricity safely to the ground, avoiding damage to the building.

PLANTS depend on nitrogen in the soil to grow and to produce their own food. There is nitrogen in the air all around us. The powerful jolt of electricity from lightning can change some of the nitrogen in air into forms that plants can use. Rain carries the usable forms of nitrogen to the ground.

THUNDERSTORMS DO MORE than create dramatic lightning and thunder. They cause strong winds called updrafts that rise quickly through the clouds. These winds can sweep away tiny particles and smelly gases that pollute the air.

How It Works

People often say they feel better, and even happier, after a thunderstorm. Part of this feeling is caused by the rain and wind clearing and cooling the air. But your mood can also be lifted by some of the electric charge remaining in the air.

YOU MIGHT NOT ENJOY getting soaked in a thunderstorm. But did you know how important that rain really is? Those heavy rains help replenish the water supplies in reservoirs. More than half of the public water supply in the United States, for example, comes from those storms.

THUNDERSTORMS often develop where there is a clash of warm and cold air. The warm air rises until moisture begins to come out of it, forming storm clouds. Once the storm develops, air cooled along the edges of the storm can come rushing down and spread out at ground level like air-conditioning.

That's better!

11

Will the Wind Ever Stop Blowing?

Wind is a constant feature of Earth's weather, either strengthening or weakening as it swirls around, or blowing steadily in one direction. The wind is caused by many things: our planet's spinning, the warmth of the sea or land below, the pressure of the air itself. Light winds are refreshing, but the most extreme winds are destructive. The strongest winds occur in tornadoes, with their terrifying swirling shape. They're powerful enough to lift cattle, automobiles, and even houses and fling them far away.

An Ill Wind

HURRICANES—also called cyclones or typhoons—are powerful storms that develop over warm seas.

A TORNADO is a column of powerfully swirling air extending from a thundercloud down to the ground.

WATERSPOUTS are versions of tornadoes that develop over water—either the ocean or lakes.

A NOR'EASTER is a powerful storm along the New England coast, with strong winds blowing from the northeast.

JET STREAMS are narrow "ribbons" of air that blow from west to east high up in the atmosphere.

SANDSTORMS develop when strong winds blow loose sand and dust into the air.

THE MISTRAL is a strong northerly wind that blows across southern France, often for days on end.

PLANTS can use the wind to help spread seeds. You can see how, by blowing on the wisps of a dandelion. Its seeds are sent off so that new plants can grow far from the parent.

You Can Do It!

Gather up some maple seeds when they're produced in the fall. They're in pairs, with each seed attached to a wing. Break them apart and toss them up in the air on a breezy day. Watch how well these "helicopters" hitch a ride on the wind—and check how far they fly.

STRONG WINDS aren't all bad. Many sports and games rely on a good breeze. Skiers can work up a good speed on level ground with the help of a parachute to capture the wind.

SPECIALLY EQUIPPED PLANES called hurricane hunters fly through hurricanes. The information they record helps weather scientists learn more about how storms develop.

13

What Is a Heat Wave?

Hot weather can turn unpleasant when it hits extremes and there's no end in sight. Meteorologists often describe a heat wave as three or more straight days when the temperature is unusually high for a particular region. Not only is this exceptional heat uncomfortable, but it can lead to serious problems. Water supplies may dry up, causing a drought.

The combination of extreme heat and dry air often breeds serious wildfires, which can sweep through forests and open country and destroy towns. Extreme threats like these wildfires often call for equally extreme responses, which may include "fighting fire with fire." Firefighters build a controlled fire, called a backfire or backburn, to burn up the trees in the path of the wildfire. This stops the wildfire in its tracks, because there is no more fuel for it to burn.

VILLAGES have sometimes been abandoned so that the land can be flooded to make a reservoir. In a long drought, when the water level is much lower than usual, parts of old buildings may become visible again.

YOU NEED WATER if you're out in the heat, especially if you are exercising. Dehydration (loss of fluid from the body) can be dangerous.

Top Tip

If you have a porch, spray it with water in hot weather. The water absorbs some of the heat as it evaporates. And with the heat taken away—at least for a while—your porch becomes cooler and more comfortable.

JUST AS APPLES and some other fruits need cold winters to thrive, some plants need to be exposed to extreme heat for their seeds to develop. Fire poppies and other flowers add color to a dry, burnt landscape.

THE DUST BOWL occurred in the 1930s when a severe drought and dust storms destroyed farming land across much of central North America. Families were forced to leave their unproductive farms.

How Cold Can It Get?

In the coldest winters, everything in nature seems to slow down or stop. And the regions near Earth's poles remain cold even in the summer. Earth's coldest temperature, –128.6 degrees Fahrenheit (89.2 degrees Celsius), was recorded at Russia's Vostok scientific station, in Antarctica, in 1983. Most of us never face temperatures nearly that cold, but some people live in areas where winters regularly dip below –40°F (–40°C). And for many of them, winter is a time for sports and celebration.

Signpost at Vostok scientific station

Cold Comfort

FARMING COMMUNITIES in Russia have always celebrated the first snowfall. Snow is welcomed because it acts as a blanket—a comforter, you might say—over the crops. It insulates the soil from the intense cold of the air.

MANY NORTHERN REGIONS have annual winter carnivals with games, snowman-building contests, and prizes for the best ice sculptures.

SOME ANIMALS are well suited to the cold, with a good coat of fur or a layer of body fat. The huskies that pull dogsleds in Alaska can tolerate temperatures as low as –70°F (–57°C).

WINTER SPORTS are popular in countries that have very cold winters. Ice hockey began as a Native American sport. Some people still play it on frozen ponds rather than skating rinks.

ORANGE TREES suffer in freezing weather. Growers often defend against cold by sprinkling water on the trees. When it freezes, it gives off some heat—maybe enough to protect the trees.

17

Is It Still Raining?

Rain—or the lack of it—is usually the first thing that comes to mind when people think about the weather. We'd much rather it didn't rain on big events like graduations or parades, or on more local occasions such as picnics or days at the beach. But many parts of the world don't just have rainy days—they have rainy seasons with daily downpours. And without those periods of extreme rain, they wouldn't be able to grow crops. Many of the world's great civilizations developed in areas where ample rain provided them with enough of the "water of life."

Thank goodness you came in time!

A SUDDEN PERIOD of heavy rain can spell disaster for people living near rivers or in valleys. Waters can rise quickly, and some people may need to be rescued from their homes by boat.

Lever

Pivot (fulcrum)

Counterweight

EGYPTIANS have relied on the waters of the Nile for thousands of years. Each spring it floods its banks, dumping rich soil on nearby farms. Some farmers still use the traditional balanced shadoof (left) to lift water from the river.

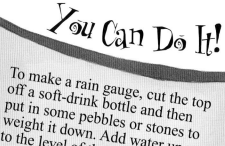

You Can Do It!

To make a rain gauge, cut the top off a soft-drink bottle and then put in some pebbles or stones to weight it down. Add water up to the level of the stones; mark this as your baseline. Tape the neck of the bottle upside down, to act as a funnel. Use a ruler and a marker pen to mark off inches or centimeters from the baseline upward.

I hope a tasty zebra comes along.

GRASSLANDS CALLED SAVANNA cover large parts of East Africa. For much of the year these treeless spaces are parched, but the rainy season brings fresh grasses and fills the water holes.

SOME OF US take water for granted, but in many parts of the world, people must walk long distances to fetch water. Often this job goes to children.

HAILSTONES DEVELOP when thunderstorms send air looping up and down quickly. Raindrops caught up in that loop freeze when they reach the top. Some of them melt and fall as rain. Others pick up more water and continue to go up and freeze over again—getting bigger and bigger until they fall as hail.

Rattle!

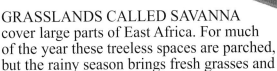

Has Extreme Weather Shaped Our World?

Even the most extreme weather boils down to two main ingredients: wind and water. But these can become fearsome weapons, eating away at soil and rock, carving huge valleys and forming some eerie shapes in the landscape. And when you add the extremes of heat and cold to the mix, this "landscaping" can become even more dramatic. Many of the world's most memorable natural features owe their appearance to the forces of the weather.

THE ALPINE VALLEYS of Switzerland were carved by glaciers during the last ice age. They are sometimes called U-shaped valleys because they have a wide floor and slightly curved sides.

Monument Valley is featured in many movies about the American West.

Months of blizzard winds whip layer upon layer of freezing sea spray against an exposed reef in the Southern Ocean near Antarctica. The result is this startling mushroom shape, which melts each summer.

DESERT HEAT, winter cold, wind, and water have carved a spectacular landscape from the sandstone of Monument Valley in Utah and Arizona. Heat and cold cause rocks to shrink and expand, forming cracks.

NEW ENGLAND'S fall explosion of colorful leaves occurs only when there is the right combination of fading sunlight, rainfall, and temperature.

WESTERLY WINDS pile up mountains of sand in the desert dunes of Namibia in southwest Africa. The winds are constantly at work, so that the dunes change shape from day to day.

A SEA STACK is a dramatic tower of rock jutting up from the ocean. Each stack was once part of the mainland, but wind-driven waves and rain have eaten away at the soil and stone connecting it to the rest of the land.

How Do People Deal With Extreme Weather?

People find ways to cope with all sorts of harsh circumstances. If they can't change the weather, then at least they can lessen the hardship it creates. That can mean finding ways to keep dry in rainy climates, cool when it's hot outside, or comfortably warm when blizzard winds blow. One solution is to retreat into a natural shelter; another is to construct buildings that can cope with the extremes. The one thing that unites all of these approaches is imagination, and the willingness to seek out new solutions.

SOME ENERGY-SAVING modern homes look almost like a return to the time when people lived in caves.

Rock walls are nature's own insulation.

Be Prepared

MANY DESERT DWELLERS wear loose white clothing to stay cooler in the hot weather. The white reflects some of the Sun's heat and the flowing clothes provide shade and space for the skin to release heat.

How It Works

Winters are so cold in Siberia that milk is sold frozen in disks like hockey pucks. People can carry their milk home in net bags and stack the frozen disks outside until they need them.

IT'S IMPORTANT to be ready for extreme weather, especially if it arrives suddenly. Schoolchildren in many parts of the United States have regular tornado drills so that they know how to keep safe if a twister approaches.

IN COLD CLIMATES, some people prefer to spend much of their time inside. This shopping mall in the chilly state of Minnesota has stores, restaurants, green spaces, and even a theme park with rides—all indoors.

WATER IS EXTREMELY PRECIOUS in many parts of the world and people are careful not to waste it. The Indian Ocean island of Mauritius has lengthy dry periods, so people build structures to capture and store rainwater.

Can We Control the Weather?

Most of us feel that there's nothing we can do about bad weather, so we might as well accept it. But what if something *could* be done to change the weather? That question has fascinated people for thousands of years. Some societies hope that rain gods and rain dances will bring much-needed water for their crops. And then, of course, there are the millions of people who wish for just the opposite—that it would stay dry for important outdoor events. Who gets to choose?

Rain clouds at 11 o'clock!

THE ORGANIZERS of the 2008 Olympics in China's capital, Beijing, prepared well to make everything go smoothly. That included trying to make sure that it rained as little as possible. Soldiers even fired rockets to seed the clouds (see "How It Works," opposite) so they would spill their rain before reaching Beijing.

SCIENTISTS might soon be able to fire lasers (focused beams of light) into thunderclouds to change the path of lightning strikes. Lightning bolts could follow the path of the laser safely to the earth, rather than striking buildings or people.

How It Works

It's possible to trigger rain in some clouds with a process called cloud seeding. The "seeds" are tiny chemical particles that are sent into clouds from planes or rockets. Water droplets form on these chemical seeds and eventually become raindrops that fall to Earth.

Path of rocket

Seeded cloud

Rain

SOME WEATHER LEGENDS are not meant to be taken seriously. The Rip Van Winkle story suggests that thunder is the sound of old Dutch ghosts bowling.

SOME WEATHER EXPERTS recommend sending reflective dust—like the kind that volcanoes produce—into the atmosphere. Reflecting away some of the Sun's heat could reduce global warming.

RUSSIA'S CAPITAL, MOSCOW, spends millions each year clearing snow from its streets. Its mayor created a stir in 2009 when he suggested seeding clouds to make the snow fall outside the city center.

What About Climate Change?

It's one thing to imagine people being able to change the weather. But we humans face a much bigger problem—and it involves the world's climate. Through its 4.5-billion-year history, Earth has had warm periods and cooler phases. Natural events such as volcanoes triggered these periods. But most scientists now agree that Earth is warming up faster than in the past—and humans are to blame.

A major cause is carbon dioxide gas building up in the atmosphere and trapping heat inside. And our fossil fuels produce vast amounts of this carbon dioxide as waste.

GLOBAL WARMING describes one of the most alarming features of climate change. With warmer temperatures, ice caps in the Arctic are melting, and many animals—such as polar bears—are losing their natural habitats.

POWER PLANTS release large amounts of carbon dioxide. One way of keeping it out of the atmosphere is to pump it beneath the sea. It can be injected deep into rock on the seabed or stored at shallower depths.

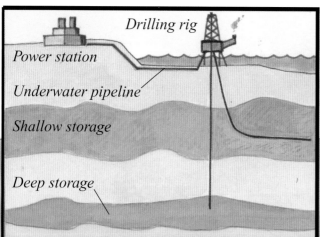

Drilling rig

Power station

Underwater pipeline

Shallow storage

Deep storage

You Can Do It!

When you turn off computers, televisions, or other electrical equipment, make sure to turn them off fully, rather than leaving them on standby. This way you use less electricity. It saves you money and saves on unnecessary carbon emissions.

MILLIONS OF PEOPLE around the world live in low-lying coastal regions. Those places face risks of flooding and even being washed away if sea levels rise just slightly because of climate change.

AS TEMPERATURES RISE, areas of rich grassland will become too hot and dry to grow very much. Deserts will creep outward to absorb lands that had once been fertile.

MAMMOTHS, huge relatives of elephants, were common for millions of years. Many scientists believe that they died out at the end of the last ice age, about 12,000 years ago. Forests replaced their natural grassland habitat as global temperatures rose.

27

How Far Can We Forecast?

Even the sky's not the limit as we look ahead to the future of weather studies. Space probes have already given us a firsthand view of weather on other planets, and ocean science on our own planet has taught us a lot. A temperature change of just a fraction of a degree in an ocean current off South America, for example, can bring downpours to New York and London. Will these new sources of knowledge help us cope better with the extremes of weather in the years ahead?

ASTRONAUTS Neil Armstrong and Buzz Aldrin landed on the Moon in 1969. The Moon lacks air and water —the main ingredients of weather— but the flag they planted was wrinkled from being packed, so it looked as though it fluttered in a breeze.

Looking Ahead

ACCURATE FORECASTS will be even more important in the future. Man-made climate change has increased the amount of extreme weather we can expect. Just a slight increase in average temperature creates more heat waves and more flooding. Hurricanes and tornadoes will become more common.

AN IMPORTANT forecasting tool is Doppler radar imaging. It uses the Doppler effect to measure the speed and direction of moving objects—in this case, clouds and storms.

You Can Do It!

The Doppler effect describes how sound waves bunch up (sound higher) as something gets closer and spread out (sound lower) as it goes away. To hear it for yourself, ask a friend to blow a whistle from the backseat of a car as it drives past you—or listen for the siren of a police car or fire truck.

CASSINI–HUYGENS, an international space probe, has found extreme weather and evidence of water on Saturn's moons.

CROWDS GATHER on February 2 to see whether groundhog Punxsutawney Phil will "predict" six more weeks of winter by seeing his shadow. But scientists are also investigating whether some animals really can detect extreme weather before it occurs.

He gets it right 39 percent of the time.

Glossary

Atmosphere The layer of gases around Earth, or around other objects in space, that gives protection from harmful radiation and keeps heat from escaping.

Blizzard A severe snowstorm that includes high winds.

Carbon dioxide A gas made up of the elements carbon and oxygen. Too much of this gas in the atmosphere can contribute to global warming.

Climate The typical weather conditions in a place or region, usually measured over a period of years.

Climate change Natural or man-made changes to the temperature of Earth and to its atmosphere, which upset normal patterns of weather over a long period.

Cyclone A large mass of swirling winds, especially one that forms in the Pacific or Indian Oceans. The same type of swirling wind is called a hurricane near North America, or a typhoon along Asia's Pacific coast.

Downpour A burst of steady, hard rain that usually lasts only a short time.

Drought A period, lasting anywhere from several weeks to a number of years, with little or no rainfall. It often leads to poor harvests and food shortages.

Dune A mound or ridge of loose sand, formed into a hilly shape by the wind.

Element One of the basic substances that cannot be separated by the use of chemistry into simpler substances.

Emissions Gases or small particles that are the waste products of engines or machinery; these are sent out (emitted) into the atmosphere and can be harmful.

Evaporate To turn from liquid to gas.

Fertile Able to produce a rich growth of plants, especially farm crops.

Fossil fuel A fuel, such as coal or oil, that is formed underground from the remains of long-dead plants and animals.

Gale A very strong wind, such as a severe storm at sea.

Glacier A large body of ice, formed from densely packed snow that slides very slowly downhill.

Global warming A gradual rise in the temperature of Earth's oceans and atmosphere, caused at least partly by human activity such as burning fossil fuels.

Habitat The place, or the type of place, where a plant or animal normally lives and reproduces.

Insulator Something that slows or stops the flow of such types of energy as electricity or heat.

Laser A beam of powerful light that remains concentrated on a small point even when projected over long distances.

Meteorologist A scientist who studies and forecasts the weather.

Nitrogen The most abundant chemical element in Earth's atmosphere. It is present in all living things.

Ozone layer The layer of Earth's atmosphere that contains the most ozone, a gas that protects us from the Sun's harmful radiation.

Probe An unmanned space vehicle sent out on a scientific mission.

Radiation A general name for different forms of energy that travel in waves, spreading outward from a source just as waves in water spread out from a splash.

Reservoir A lake—usually artificially created but sometimes natural—where water is collected and stored. The water is often carried long distances by pipeline to the place where it is needed.

Satellite An unmanned space vehicle launched to go into orbit around Earth.

Index

Building to Beat the Weather

Extreme weather can be a problem when it catches us by surprise. But in areas that have an extreme climate, it is possible to plan ahead. Houses and other buildings can be designed to cope with the kinds of weather that are likely to occur.

Many houses in coastal areas are built on stilts. You enter them by climbing a ladder, which you can then pull up after you. If heavy waves or coastal floods raise the water level, the people in the houses remain "high and dry." Stilt houses in hot countries also allow cool breezes to flow through in all directions. Houses of this kind have been built for thousands of years, since the late Stone Age.

People living in some of the coldest parts of Alaska also raise their houses on stilts, but for a different reason. Some of those places get enough snow to bury an ordinary one-story house, so it's important to be above the snow level as it rises through the winter.

There are other ways to carve living space from what nature provides. People living in the hotter parts of Spain, France, and Turkey often burrow into soft stone to build cave houses. Halls and tunnels connect different rooms, and the temperature inside is stable throughout the seasons.

These houses are used all year round, but the ice hotels in Scandinavia and other places have to be rebuilt each winter. Even the beds are made from blocks of ice, although they're covered with thick blankets and bedspreads.

Weather Satellites

The first successful weather satellite was TIROS-1, launched by the National Aeronautics and Space Administration (NASA) in 1960. It sent information about cloud cover and movement back to Earth, to help with weather forecasting. Since then, dozens of satellites have been launched, and not just by the United States. The European Space Agency, Russia, China, India, and Japan have all sent satellites into Earth orbit.

Some satellites remain fixed over a particular part of Earth, along the equator (the imaginary line around Earth that separates the Northern and Southern Hemispheres). Others follow a pole-to-pole orbit that means that over time they look down on every part of the planet. These satellites have become more and more advanced over the years. Once, they simply kept a lookout for storms and clouds. Now, they also record temperatures and the condition of the atmosphere, and provide information to scientists studying climate change.

In just over five decades, satellite technology has enabled scientists to pinpoint some of the causes of extreme weather and to study the full effects that humans have had on the climate. Such information is vital to allow governments to plan for the future.